Just Like Mike

For Jeff, as always

Just Like Mike

Gail Herman

HOUGHTON MIFFLIN

BOSTON

Houghton Mifflin Edition

Printed in China

ISBN–13: 978-0-618-93255-9
ISBN–10: 0-618-93255-0

1 2 3 4 5 6 7 8 9 SDP 15 14 13 12 11 10 09 08

CHAPTER

"We love Michael!"

"Hurray for Michael Jordan!"

People are shouting and cheering, and it's all for me, Michael Jordan. Other basketball players slap me on the back, thrilled to be on the same court as me.

I toss the ball and *swish!* Just like always, it's a perfect shot.

Reporters rush over while the TV cameras roll. What should I say this time?

"Over here, Michael!" the reporters call. "Michael! Michael Jordan!"

"Michael!" calls another voice. "Michael Jordan! Have you finished packing?"

The basketball turns into a wad of paper.

The basket is a bowl.

Those aren't reporters calling me.

It's my mom.

And those cheers and shouts aren't for me. They're for the real Michael Jordan—the basketball star. He's making an appearance at a basketball game on TV. And I'm in my living room, watching.

I toss the paper into the bowl. And just like always, I miss.

My friend Jim laughs. "Almost got it!" he says. "And why is your mom calling you Michael Jordan already? Your name doesn't change until after the wedding."

"She's just practicing," I tell Jim.

I've been doing that for weeks now too—calling myself Michael Jordan. We're both trying to see what it will be like when it really is my name—once and for all.

I think it will be pretty darn awful.

But at least for now, I'm still Michael Brown. Plain old Michael Brown—until Mom marries Mr. Jordan, that is. And then the name Michael Jordan?

That will be as real as real can be.

If only I was like the real Michael Jordan, I wouldn't mind having his name. But I'm short and chubby, so I look more like a basketball than a basketball star.

"But you can't play basketball without a ball," I say, trying to feel better.

Mom walks into the room. She flips off the TV. Michael Jordan's face disappears.

"Michael," says Mom. "I asked you a question. Did you finish packing? The movers will be here any minute."

"Yes, I'm all done," I answer. "The boxes are all in my room." I swallow. "I mean my old room."

"Good." Mom smiles. "I know this is hard, becoming part of a new family and moving to a new town. But I think it will work out great." She flips the TV back on. "I'll let you get back to the game. I know how much you love basketball."

Basketball players race up and down the court. Jim cheers as a player scores.

Sure, I love basketball. I love to watch it. And I love to dream that I'm a great player.

But playing—I mean really playing—I'm not too sure about.

A few minutes later, Jim says, "Good-bye," and I feel a little sniffly.

"Good-bye," I say, wanting to hug him but only shaking hands.

I go up to my room for one last look. It's all so strange. The walls are bare, and boxes fill the floor. I spy my wastebasket in one corner, and some rumpled-up newspaper used for packing in another.

"Why not try another shot?" I ask myself. I toss a newspaper ball just as the doorbell rings. "He beats the buzzer!" I shout. Then I sigh, because of course I miss. And it's the movers at the door, ready to take all this away.

A few minutes later, some guys shuffle in and begin to move our stuff. Then we

get into our car and drive to our new house.

Tomorrow is the wedding, and tonight I toss and turn.

The bed feels strange.

The shadows look strange.

I can't sleep at all.

A new family. A new dad. Mr. Jordan.

Oops, I'm supposed to call him Dad.

But what about my real dad? He died years ago. I don't remember him at all—just a kind of smell, of outdoors and wet grass, reminds me of him sometimes. But do I just forget him altogether? Forget everything about my old life?

At the wedding, Mom looks so happy, I try to look happy too. But she knows something is wrong. She pulls me away from the party.

"Honey," she says. "Are you all right?"

Before I can answer, Mr. Jordan—oops, I mean Dad—hurries over too.

"Is everything okay, sport?"

Mr. Jordan calls me "sport" a lot. He thinks it's funny because of my new name. Sometimes I try to laugh too. This time, I can't even try. I mean, I like Mr. Jordan and all. I really do—he watches basketball with me. He talks to me about school and friends and lots of different things. But do I love him like a father?

No—at least, not yet.

"Is everything okay?" Mr. Jordan asks again.

It's hard to put everything into words. So I just say what I always say about the marriage.

"I don't want to be Michael Jordan.

Michael Jordan is the best basketball player ever, and I'm the worst. People will laugh and make fun of me. I can't be Michael Jordan!"

Mom shakes her head like she's done before. "I want us to be a family," she says. "A family with the same last name."

Mr. Jordan puts his arm around me. I glance up at him and think maybe he'll understand.

"But there are so many new things to get used to," I tell him. "It's not just my name—it's going to a new school with my new name."

Mr. Jordan squeezes my shoulder. "It won't be so bad," he tells me. "It will be the first day of school for everyone. Your mom and I planned our wedding so you can start school in September, along with all the other kids. Besides, we're all in this together. We're a family. And we'll all take things one day at a time."

I think this over as Mom and Mr. Jordan get ready to leave the party. Guests gather confetti to throw, and I take a handful.

"A new school," I repeat slowly. Hey, maybe that won't be too bad. I didn't have many friends at my old school. Just Jim.

Maybe this is my chance.

Maybe kids will think my name is cool.

Maybe they'll think I'm cool.

I toss the confetti at Mom and Mr. Jordan and miss by a mile.

Maybe not.

CHAPTER 2

It's the first day of school and all around me, kids are talking and laughing. I pretend I'm happy to be alone. I try to smile, but I'm too nervous to do even that. Finally the bell rings and we file into classrooms.

In my room, the teacher takes attendance. I sneak looks at the other third-graders. What will they think when she says "Michael Jordan"?

"Sara Gibbs . . . Ben Harris . . . ," the teacher calls.

Here it comes . . .

"Michael Jordan?"

"Michael Jordan?" kids repeat. Already they're laughing.

"Here," I squeak from the back row.

All the kids whip around. They see me, and they laugh even harder.

I swallow hard and pretend to be interested in a map on the wall.

"Quiet down, class," Ms. Wood says.

I spy our state on the map. Then I see Australia way on the other side. I wish I could be in Australia—as far away from here as I can get.

After school, I walk by the schoolyard and see a basketball game. I know I should keep walking. Hanging around a basketball court when your name is Michael Jordan and you look like a basketball is just asking for trouble.

But I can't help it. The game is exciting, and I have to stop and watch. A kid from my class makes a perfect shot. His name is Tim, and he's tall and thin. *He* should be called Michael Jordan.

"Hey, everybody," Tim shouts. "Look who's here! Michael Jordan!"

Everyone gasps and looks around.

They don't see a basketball star.

They see me.

"If that's Michael Jordan," a boy says, "I'm president of the United States."

A few kids snicker, and a girl says, "Good one, Terry!"

"Come on," Tim tells them. "Give the guy a chance." He holds out the ball. "Dunk, Mike!"

Everyone laughs at short, chubby me.

I try to laugh too, but I wind up coughing instead. When I finish, everybody is waiting.

"Dunk, Mike, dunk!" they shout.

My heart beats fast. I want to go home—back to my other home. The one we lived in before I became Michael Jordan. It wasn't so great being plain old Michael Brown. But it was better than this.

Suddenly I remember the basketball dream I had while I watched TV. The cheering fans and the players putting me on their shoulders. "Michael, Michael, Michael," I hear.

Just like in the dream, I step forward. I take the ball and bounce it. Once. Twice. Everyone is quiet. This is my chance.

"You can do it," I tell myself. "You can dunk."

I grip the ball tight and leap high into the air. I use two hands and jam it . . . right into a garbage pail!

"You stink," Terry crows. "Just like this garbage!"

Everyone laughs louder than ever. I try to smile and laugh it off. But no one is watching anymore, so I slink quietly away.

What a way to start a new school.

CHAPTER 3

The next day, it seems everyone knows my name.

"That's Michael Jordan," a girl whispers in gym class.

Tim and Terry and a bunch of friends are tossing a basketball at one side of the gym. I decide to stay on the other side. I dribble a basketball across the floor—right onto my foot.

"Oh," says the girl to a friend. "Poor

guy. Imagine if your name was Michael Jordan and you couldn't play basketball to save your life."

"Hey, Michael," she calls. "Would you like to jump rope with us?"

I see Tim and Terry turn around to look. "Ha, ha," I say to make it into a joke. "Me? Jump rope? Not when I can play basketball!" Then I hurry away, and stay in the bathroom for the rest of class.

I wish those girls would make fun of me instead of trying to be nice. That's way worse!

Somehow I make it through the day— and the next couple of days too. I try not to talk to anyone so no one will talk to me. I rush right home after school. I hang out in the bathroom during gym, and I eat lunch in a dark corner of the schoolyard while everyone else plays basketball.

On Friday afternoon, I crawl into bed. One week down, I think. Only forty-two left to go before summer.

"I hate everything," I say out loud. My new school . . . my new family. If only I wasn't Michael Jordan, everything would be easy.

Then I hear Mr. Jordan—I mean Dad— come into the house.

"What's wrong, Michael?" he asks, knocking at my door. "Should I call your mom at work? Are you sick?"

"I'm sick of being Michael Jordan," I tell him. Then it all comes out. How I hate my name, my school, and everything else.

Dad listens carefully—I can see him thinking hard when I talk about my basketball goofs and trying to laugh everything off.

"Well," he says, "it sounds like you're

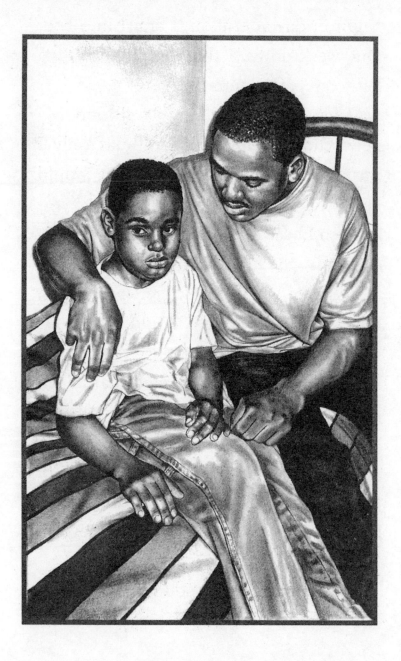

doing the best you can—making a joke and keeping it light. Maybe you should do that even more. As for your name—we can't change it back. You know how your mom and I feel about that." He smiles and gives me a hug. "But maybe we can change something else."

CHAPTER 4

Monday morning at school, I feel better. Not great, mind you. Better. I hear more kids whisper and laugh. "There goes Michael Jordan!"

I laugh along, like Dad told me to keep doing—like it's all a funny joke. And now I take it even further. "Wait till you see my new sneaker commercial," I say with a smile.

All morning long I make jokes about

my name. But I'm not sure anyone else is laughing. At lunch, I decide to eat in the cafeteria, where everyone can hear my jokes.

Tim follows me to a table. "You've been a riot these last couple of days," he tells me. "That dunk into the garbage pail? And the dribble off your foot? Boy, those were funny."

Tim thinks my basketball playing has been a joke too—just like all the cracks I've been making!

"But why do you keep running off when we play basketball after school?" he asks.

I have to think quickly now. Why do I leave? Why? Why? Why? "I have to go home and feed the dog," I blurt out. We don't even have a dog.

"Really?" says Tim.

A crowd gathers around to listen.

I nod and add, "I'm really a very good player." My voice sounds normal. But inside, my stomach is twisted into knots. I've never lied like this before—first a dog, and now my playing. If I keep going, I'll say I'm the real Michael Jordan any minute now.

"Well, we play basketball practically every day," Tim says. "We could use another guy."

"Yeah! Great idea!" the other kids shout.

"I can't make it," I say quickly. But nobody pays attention. They're all making plans.

"We'll have the best team ever," Tim says. "We have Michael Jordan!"

CHAPTER 5

I wish I could get out of it, but I can't think of a way. So after school I go to the basketball court. I stand around, feeling nervous. There must be twenty kids here, watching. Terry points to the garbage pail and laughs. My heart pounds and my hands sweat. How will I even hold the ball?

"Come on, Mike," says Tim. "Show us what you've got. Dunk!" He tosses the ball to me. Surprise, surprise. I catch it.

I look at the basket and remember that old daydream. I can almost hear the fans. The cheers of "Michael, Michael, Michael!" Quickly I shake my head. Thinking like that doesn't help. I know that for a fact.

But then I remember something else: playing hoops with Dad over the weekend. It was the very first time we played, and Dad showed me some pretty good moves. Mom joined in too, and we all shot the ball around.

We practiced for hours. And we felt like a family. The Jordan family. I smile just thinking about it, because it was even better than my dream.

My heart slows down and my hands are not so sweaty. I dribble the ball, then take off. I jump high, just like Dad showed me—just like Michael Jordan.

Up I go. Up, up, up. *Whoosh*—I jam the ball. Basket!

Terry gives a long, low whistle. People cheer and shout as I tumble to the ground. "That was great, Mike!" says Tim. "You can be on our team anytime!"

Play on a real live basketball team? Not just in a dream? I put everything I had into that one dunk. Could I, Michael Jordan, play a real game? Now? No! I need more practice. I need more help from Dad.

How can I get out of this? "Ouch!" I shout. "My ankle!" It *is* twisted for real. Tim and Terry put me on their shoulders. I feel like a real sports hero as they carry me back to my new home. And my new dad.

Right away, Mom and Dad take me to the doctor. It's not too bad. All I need is a bandage—and some rest. Still, I talk Dad

into shooting hoops when we get home. "I'll be careful," I promise.

My ankle hurts, but not too bad. I'm hoping I'll be playing basketball with Tim. Soon.

Uh-oh. I miss shot after shot. Well, maybe not *that* soon.

CHAPTER 6

Weeks have passed. My amazing dunk is history. And my twisted ankle? That's history too. Tim hasn't talked about the basketball team again—we've been busy doing other things. We go to the movies and out for ice cream and ride bikes around the neighborhood. Terry comes along too sometimes, and some other kids from school. We never go to my house, though. What if they ask about my dog? The one I don't have?

We all have fun. But just in case basket-ball comes up, I still limp every once in a while. I can always say I have to feel better before I play. Then one day, I feel so good—about Tim, me, and everything—I decide to tell him the truth. That I don't have a dog. Or a limp.

"Hey, Mike!" Tim bounds over on the way to school.

"Hi, Tim," I say. "I have to tell you some-thing—"

"I have something to tell you, too!" Tim interrupts. "My dad is starting a Little League team! And we're all going to play!"

Little League? Baseball? What happened to hoops?

"But what about those basketball games?" I ask.

Tim shrugs. "We haven't played in so long, it doesn't really matter. Besides, we can play again after baseball season."

Then he slaps me on the back. "What position do you play? Outfield, like Michael Jordan did?"

"Uh . . . uh . . . I guess so," I stammer.

Tim laughs. "We can still tell everybody we have Michael Jordan! And he left basketball to play baseball for our team. It will be great!"

Then Tim gives me a look. "You can play baseball, can't you?"

"Sure," I say quickly. "Just as well as basketball!"

Well, that's the absolute truth. I stink at both. I'm about to explain, to tell Tim everything, but before I say a word, he hurries away. I can hear him clear across the schoolyard, telling kids about the team—and its star player, Michael Jordan.

Who knows? Maybe, just maybe, I can be a star. Quick, I think, suddenly excited. Call ESPN and every sports reporter in town. Stop the presses. Michael Jordan gives up basketball. Michael Jordan signs on for baseball. Then I sigh, remembering everything.

Too bad this Michael Jordan can't play *any* sport.

CHAPTER 7

It's dinnertime, and Mom and Dad are talking about some big surprise.

Who cares? I ask myself. I've got bigger things to think about. I frown at the table, worrying about bats, balls, and gloves.

"What's wrong, Michael?" asks Mom. "Does your ankle hurt again?"

"I'm fine," I say. I don't look up. I don't want Mom and Dad to see me upset again.

"Do you want to shoot hoops after dinner?" Dad asks. "We can work on defense."

"No thanks," I say. I stare so hard at my soup bowl, I count every single pea. Over my head, I know Mom and Dad are looking at each other.

What's wrong? they think. What's eating Michael now?

"All right, all right! I'll tell you!" I burst out. I jump out of my seat.

Mom and Dad look surprised. But maybe that's because my soup is all over the floor.

I sponge and talk at the same time. "There's going to be a Little League team," I explain. "And I can't play baseball!"

In a flash, Mom and Dad take me outside. The kitchen floor is still sticky, but I guess they don't care. They find a bat and

ball in the garage, and before I know it, I'm standing on a pizza box home plate, ready to swing.

"Okay," Mom says. "Take it easy. Wait for the right pitch."

She tosses the ball to me, nice and slow. Piece of cake, I think. A baby can hit this. I swing with all my might and miss. My body twists and I fall to the ground.

"Yeah," I say out loud. "Piece of cake—*fruitcake*. And I'm a fruitcake to think I could ever play!"

CHAPTER 8

The next day we have practice. Terry is there, of course, and some kids from school.

Terry elbows me in the ribs. "This is so great!" he says. "Michael Jordan gives up basketball to play baseball. I bet real reporters come to our games!"

I remember that dream I had before the wedding. About reporters crowding around, asking questions. Of course, that

would be great. But it's not really important. My new friends are important—and
I'm worried about keeping them!

Tim's dad hurries over.

"Say, Mike!" he says. "How about bat-
ting a few?"

Great, I'm up first. Tim steps on the
pitcher's mound. I take the bat and hold it
over my head. I pretend to stretch. I tap
my feet with the bat. Then I stretch again.
I figure I can do this for five more minutes.
Then I'm sunk.

At the mound, Tim waves at me. He's
ready to start. I get into position—at least,
what I think is position.

Suddenly a horn honks. It's Mom!

"Michael!" she calls, and opens the car
door. A big puppy comes running out. Dog?
We don't have a dog. But what a way out!

I slap my head like I forgot something. "Oops!" I say. "I have to take care of that dog again. See you guys later!"

I race to the car and pull the dog in with me.

"This is Buster," Mom explains as he licks my face. "He's the surprise we tried to tell you about at dinner. But you didn't have to leave the game. We would have waited."

"That's okay," I tell her. "I want to go home and practice." And get to know my new dog!

CHAPTER 9

All that evening, Mom and Dad and I practice. Buster watches and helps fetch the balls.

The next day I feel ready. Well, almost ready. I stand at the plate. All at once, someone snaps my picture. A real photographer with a real reporter!

"Michael Jordan?" says the reporter. "We heard there was a boy here named Michael Jordan, and we thought it would make a nice human-interest story. Care to say a few words?"

I think a moment. If I talk long enough, maybe it will get dark. Maybe everybody will go home for dinner. But I have nothing to say, so I shake my head.

"Let's go, Mike!" Tim calls. He winds up for the pitch. Kids stand in the field, ready to catch the ball. I hunch over, keeping an eye on the ball, just like Mom showed me.

Tim lets it fly. I wait a moment, then I swing. *Crack!* I connect! I can't believe it, so I stand still.

"Run!" Terry shouts. "Run!"

I run and look for the ball at the same time. How far did it go? Not very. I see the shortstop getting ready to throw. The first baseman catches it just as I run past.

Am I safe or out?

Nobody knows. There isn't an umpire. It's only practice.

The reporter waves me over, so I jog off the field.

"Not bad," he tells me. "You could use a little power. But even Michael Jordan had off days in baseball."

I grin. Maybe I can do this, I think as I take my place in the field. Maybe I can play baseball just like Michael Jordan did.

A ball whizzes by my head. But I'm so deep in thought, it flies right past.

"Hey, Mike!" Terry shouts. "Get some glasses!"

Maybe not.

CHAPTER 10

That night, I don't practice. Not basket-ball, not baseball. I watch TV with Buster and think everything over. Do I even want to play basketball?

I wonder.

Do I even want to play baseball? And if I don't play, what will Tim say? Will he still be my friend? I can't come up with an answer. And it doesn't help that Michael Jordan is on every TV channel.

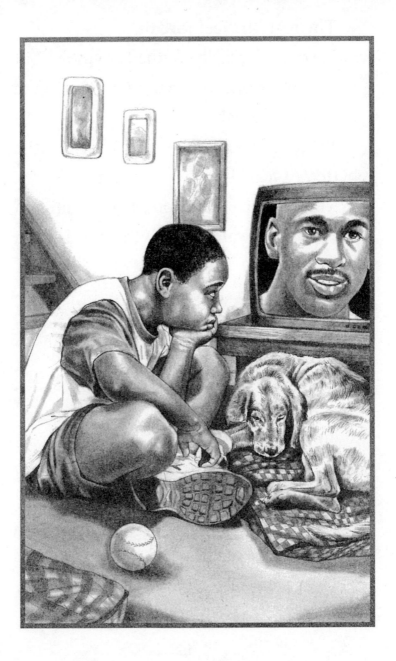

The real Michael Jordan.

He doesn't play basketball anymore. But he's still in commercials. On the news. Even in a movie!

Buster licks my face, and I feel a little better. At least I have one friend.

The next day at school, I walk through the hall to the cafeteria. On the way, I spot a sign.

TRYOUTS FOR SCHOOL PLAY THIS AFTERNOON!

It makes me remember Michael Jordan on TV—acting in a movie, in commercials. It makes me remember how I've been acting all along.

Acting like I can play basketball.

Acting like I can play baseball.

Hmmmm, I think. This could be something. This could be the answer!

Then I remember something else. Michael Jordan quit baseball to go back to basketball. He figured out what he really wanted to do. Maybe I can too.

At lunch, I sit next to Tim, just like I've been doing for weeks now.

"Hey, Mike," he says. "What's up?"

"I don't think I can join the Little League team," I tell him. "I might be too busy."

"Oh?" says Tim. He puts down his sandwich, surprised. "What's going on?"

For a very long moment, I don't say anything at all. Tim is so into sports—into basketball and baseball. If I tell him what I want to do, I bet he'll think it's strange.

Tim nudges me. "Well," he says, "what's more important than baseball?"

"Just let me take a bite of my sandwich," I say, "and then I'll tell you." I chomp down on my chicken salad on whole wheat.

Suddenly I pretend to gag. I clutch my throat. "Chicken bone," I gasp—and race out of the cafeteria.

All afternoon in class, Tim passes me notes and tries to find out what's going on.

"Why are you quitting baseball?" he whispers.

I just shake my head, making believe I'm so busy with fractions, I don't have time to answer.

When the school bell rings, I race out of the room—just like I did when school first started.

But now I don't run home. I run to the auditorium for play tryouts.

I'm just walking through the double

doors when I feel a hand on my shoulder. Tim.

"So that's it!" he says in a shocked voice. "You're trying out for the play."

I shake his hand loose. "So what?" I say gruffly, and continue inside.

Who cares what he thinks? I ask myself. But I'm not convinced. I give my name to the teacher in charge, Mr. Nichols. Then I wait my turn.

"Okay, Mike," says Mr. Nichols. "Please read from this script."

I read the part quickly. The play is about a boy named Jed and his dog, Buddy, and how they find their way home after a long, tough journey. It's like me and Buster— only with a long, tough journey. It should be easy!

"Here, boy!" I read out loud, pretending

to call a dog. "How about coming for a bike ride to the country?"

When I finish my lines, I look up.

"Nice job," says Mr. Nichols. "I'll be posting the parts tomorrow afternoon. Look for a list by the auditorium doors."

I nod and step off the stage—and see Tim waiting.

"Wow!" he says. "That was cool. You were really good!" He smiles, and we walk out together, side by side.

The next afternoon, Tim is still by my side when I check the list.

"I'm Jed!" I shout. "I got the best part!"

It's the night of the school play.

The auditorium is dark, but I know every seat is filled. My parents are in the audience, and so are Tim and Terry and practically everyone I know.

I peek through the curtain and hear the band tune up. The play is about to start.

And me—short, chubby Michael Jordan—I'm the star!

My stomach feels strange. Not like I'm

going to throw up. But close. Still, it's a different kind of nervous. Not what I feel when I'm at bat or on the free-throw line.

I know I can act. And I can't wait to get onstage.

I step back.

The curtains part.

A spotlight hits my face, and I begin to speak.

Then Buster bounds onstage—he's playing Buddy—and I really get into the part.

"You're my best buddy," I tell "Buddy" a little later, scratching his ears. "And don't worry. We'll make it back home—together."

Before I know it, the show is almost over. It all went so quickly, I can barely remember a thing. But now it's time for my last line: "Oh, Buddy," I say, leaning over to hug Buster. "We're home."

I think about Mom and Dad and Tim in the audience and Buster right beside me. And I know it's true—I am home. The curtain comes down, and the lights blink off. For a moment, we're in darkness, and I wonder: Did it really happen? Did I really act onstage? But then the lights come on, and I hear people cheer.

I slip out, to the other side of the curtain, and I see everybody standing and clapping. Mom. Dad. Tim. Terry. All the kids in my class. They're shouting for me.

"Michael Jordan!"

Somebody pushes me forward, and I take a bow with Buster.

It's almost like a dream . . . my Michael

Jordan basketball dream ... but I know this time it's for real.

And my new family, my new school, my new friends?

They're for real too.

"Hurray for Michael Jordan," I whisper, feeling glad.

About the Author

Gail Herman is the author of many books for children, including the Fairy School series. Just like Mike, she finds playing basketball and baseball no easy feat . . . but she prefers writing to acting. She lives with her husband and children in Massachusetts.